PARENTING KIDS WITH CANCER:
A Comprehensive Plan on how to handle kids with cancer.

Felix Elizabeth

All rights reserved. No. part of this publication may be produced, distributed or transmitted in a form or by any means, including photocopying,recording,or other electronic or mechanical methods, without the prior written permission of the publisher. , except in the case of brief quotations embodied in a critical review and certain other noncommercial uses permitted by copyright law.

Copyright © Felix Elizabeth,2022.

Table of contents

Chapter 1

How to allow and let go of grief

Sensations of stress can appear in changed ways for various individuals. At times, inner strain arises because circumstances in our lives don't match our inward assumptions, or because things don't go according to our arrangement.

Throughout the long term, I have discovered that this interior pressure can happen all the more serious for people who have higher self-adequacy and an inside locus of control.

We characterize self-viability as sincere confidence in our capacity to meet our objectives. The Interior locus of control connects with accepting life results are an option for us. This is something contrary to the outer locus of control, where one normally accepts that life results and circumstances are beyond one's control.

On the off chance that you are somebody who distinguishes as having areas of strength for viability and an inside locus of control, then, at that point, this can be both a positive and a negative. The positive side of this is that we effectively act such that moves us towards what we want, and we have areas of strength in our capacity to do so effectively. In any case, the negative side of this is that since we immovably accept we have some control over the results in our lives, we can get overpowered when circumstances are beyond our control. This thought can connect with both little and more critical cases in our lives, whether that is being stranded in rush hour gridlock, losing employment because of an organization cutting back, or something impeding getting an individual objective.

At the point when circumstances like these happen, it is fundamental for training the care guideline of giving up. That's what this guideline expresses on the off chance that we can figure out how to relinquish assumptions or whatever isn't in our most elevated great, the more joyful we will be. This connects with one more care standard of acknowledgment, which suggests that we want to acknowledge what is to push ahead. Assembling these two standards implies that when life circumstances happen that are not what we expected, we want to take what is and given up to push ahead. On the off chance that we don't do this, and on second thought grip to the pessimistic sensations of our assumptions not being met, it keeps us from pushing ahead and developing a more sure future. That being said, the more we can give up sincerely and push ahead when life doesn't go as expected, the more joyful and more satisfied we will be for the long haul.

Assuming the care standards of acknowledgment and giving up are difficult to try, here are a few basic procedures to help en route.

1. Allow YOURSELF TO FEEL AND Acknowledge

As circumstances emerge that didn't go as you trusted, it is fundamental to acknowledge what is happening happened, that it was beyond your control, and feel the normal close-to-home reactions. Honor the sentiments that surface first before whatever else. License yourself to feel disheartened, lament, lash out, or vent to friends and family. It is urgent to permit yourself to feel what you feel without judgment or analysis. Do whatever it takes not to be too severe with yourself as you feel a characteristic profound reaction.

2. Choose WHEN TO Give up

As you notice these feelings, let yourself know what time allotment you will permit yourself to have this impression, and when you will give up and push ahead. For instance, perhaps you will allow yourself an hour daily for the following seven days, or give yourself an entire 24 hours to feel disheartened or miserable. Consider yourself responsible for anything that period you set. Let yourself know that after the period you select elapses, you will push ahead.

3. Make A Confirmation

While remembering the picked period, make an assertion that connects with tolerating what is happening and giving up. For example, "I acknowledge that X happened, and I will push ahead," or "I will be more joyful once I acknowledge that this was beyond my control and make strides towards my next objective."

Indispensable to make an insistence impact on you. To assist the insistence with staying, get it on paper, or put it someplace, you will see it routinely.

For more on certification-type rehearses, see Ways Of show.

4. PRACTICE Over the long run.

The following stage is to begin to utilize the affirmation(s) to give up. This step can be hard because the brain will need to ruminate and continue to contemplate what turned out poorly. Once more, the sentiments could come up. This is where consistency is fundamental. Keep on utilizing the affirmation(s) each time the sentiments arise and keep rehearsing this step over the long run. Practice, practice, practice to continue to give up.

5. Keep in mind "Giving up" IS A Decision

Advise yourself that giving up is a decision. Giving up is deciding not to permit what is irritating you to do so any longer. It is relinquishing anything that no longer serves the best version of yourself or your best aims. Use the self-adequacy and inner locus of control for your potential benefit.

6. NOTICE THE POSITIVE OF Giving up.

To wrap things up, it's significant to perceive the positive effect that tolerance and giving up has on one's close-to-home prosperity. Notice what it seems like to not clutch outrage or bitterness. Notice how it enthusiastically lets loose you push ahead. The more this can be perceived; the more uplifting feedback will assist with proceeding with this way of behaving.

By and large, giving up is hard for some individuals, and it takes practice to become adept at it. Like anything more throughout everyday life, the more one practices, the more capable the individual will get at rehearsing acknowledgment and giving up. Generally speaking, the more we can give up and push ahead when things don't go as expected, the more joyful and more satisfied we will

How to be supportive of the kids

Instructions to be steady to messes with malignant growth

Hearing that your youngster has malignant growth is alarming for any parent. Today, most youth malignant growth patients can hope to have full and useful lives. Numerous youth malignant growth survivors return to school, go to school, enter the labor force, wed, and become guardians. By the by, being watchful about follow-up care, monitoring long haul and late impacts of treatment, assisting your youngster with getting back to school, and in any event, managing your feelings are everything you'll have to make due.

Focusing on Children and Young People with Blood Diseases:

You are probably going to encounter a large number of feelings from the time your kid is determined to have the disease, all through treatment and then some. These feelings might incorporate shock, disavowal, dread, outrage, culpability, and bitterness. You might feel that life for your kid and family won't ever go back. Permit yourself to feel miserable. Comprehend that you are not to fault for your kid's conclusion. Over the long haul, you'll track down ways of adjusting and continuously foster another feeling of predictability for yourself as well as your loved ones.

These sentiments are normal, yet assuming you feel consumed by sentiments or can't work, look for proficient assistance. Therapists, social specialists, and profound consultants may likewise assist you with grappling with your kid's conclusion. It's critical to deal with your sentiments so you can assist your kid with adapting and you can keep on overseeing different parts of day-to-day life and work.

Conversing with Your Kid About Their Analysis
Notwithstanding age, youngsters are generally mindful when their well-being causes their folks concern. Your youngster might encounter various feelings, like resentment, responsibility, dread, uneasiness, and bitterness, all with hardly a pause in between.

A few guardians wish to protect their youngsters from data about the sickness and its therapy. Remember that your kid will utilize their creative mind to fill in what the person in question sees as holes in data. Sharing data about the sickness and therapy assists your kid with building trust in both you and the individuals from the therapy group so the person in question feels open to discussing fears and concerns. Urge your youngster to discuss their interests and seek clarification on pressing issues.

Acquaint your kid with treatment colleagues who give psychosocial support, like a therapist, nurturer, social laborer, and youngster life subject matter expert. As well as assisting you with clearing up the ailment and its treatment for your kid, they can assist your kid with bettering figure out their sickness through play or different exercises.

For offspring of all ages, assuming you notice alarming changes in mindset or conduct, connect with the medical services group for help.

Conversing with Your Youngster About Disease

Ways Of assisting Your Youngster With adapting
It will assist your kid with adapting to their conclusion on the off chance that you:

Give design to expand your youngster's feeling of control. Kids need structure in their current circumstances. Make things as steady as could be expected. For instance, plan a standard schedule that you will keep during your time together in the medical clinic or facility.
Recognize and commend your kid when the individual in question is doing troublesome things. Irregular recognition is the most ideal way to support the helpful ways of behaving that you need to find in your kid.
Utilize similar ramifications for a terrible or unseemly way of behaving as you did before your kid was determined to have the disease. Consistency will keep up with construction and predictability.
Show that you regard your kid's outrage, stress, trouble, or dread. Give your kid a suitable source for communicating these sentiments, like drawing or keeping a diary.
Keep your kid occupied with exercises during treatment to take their brain off troublesome and upsetting encounters.
Assist your kid with remaining associated with companions from home and school with calls, messages, or visits, if conceivable.
Request proficient help for your youngster if the person is having a particularly troublesome time changing by the disease determination and its treatment.

Kin
At the point when a kid is determined to have malignant growth, everybody in their family is impacted by the experience, including the kid's family. For tips on assisting youngsters with adapting to a kin's determination, click here.

School
Most kids who have the disease will go to class, in any event, a portion of the time, both during and after their treatment. You'll have to guarantee that your youngster's schooling is begun, kept up with, or changed on a case-by-case basis. Let your youngster's teachers, medical caretakers, and life mentors understand what's going on. School is a spot for gaining and fun so youngsters benefit from getting back to their homerooms when medicinally conceivable. However, getting back to school after malignant growth treatment can be an extreme change for youthful survivors.

To look into getting back to school and projects that can make the change more straightforward for yourself as well as your kid, click here.

Long haul and Late Impacts of Life as a youngster Disease
Therapy for youth blood disease implies gambles for the long haul and late impacts that might influence

Learning (mental impacts)
Actual turn of events
Ripeness (capacity to have natural youngsters)
Mental turn of events
Hazard of an optional malignant growth.
Explicit impacts rely on the youngster's age, orientation, kind of treatment, and extra factors. The reach and seriousness of potential long haul and late impacts differ. A few youngsters will make no huge impacts or extremely gentle impacts, others might have serious confusion.

In any case, early meditation and a solid way of life rehearsal (not smoking, great sustenance, working out, normal screenings, and follow-up care) can assist with diminishing the event or potential seriousness of any late impacts.

Ask your kid's treatment group the accompanying inquiries:

What signs or side effects demonstrate a long haul or late impact?
Who would it be a good idea for me to contact if my youngster fosters any of these side effects?
How might we diminish the probability or seriousness of long haul or late impacts?
Could you at any point give printed arrangements of potential impacts and signs or side effects? What are the conceivable long haul and late impacts my youngster might insight?Might you at any point give a rundown screening tests and when they ought to begin (for instance, a mammogram)?

Chapter 2

Be a compassionate parent

Instructions to Become an Empathetic Parent

There are many advantages to figuring out how to feel your feelings. One is it assists you with turning into a more humane, compassionate parent.

The prior weekend I traveled to Iceland, I hauled my baggage out of our extra space and ran over the crates I'm putting something aside for my young ladies. These crates contain my girls' all are specialty, birthday enrichments, cards, journals, and so forth, from the time they were young ladies.

It was a family end of the week, so we as a whole chose to go through these mementos together. It was a sweet encounter, yet in addition, a miserable one when my girl, Sabrina, found a diary she'd written in primary school. While reciting a couple of pages without holding back, she was overwhelmed with excruciating recollections. She had composed this diary when I was so occupied with my life that she had felt undetectable.

Sabrina was set off by this excruciating memory and communicated it. As you can envision, it was difficult so I could hear. Yet rather than responding protectively, I sat with her and let her deal with it.

Nurturing is difficult for overcomers of youngster misuse. At the point when my young ladies were in grade school, I hadn't begun my recuperating venture. I was as yet caught in my injury. In those days, I was unable to permit them to communicate their agonizing sensations of profound deserting. Be that as it may, presently I can.

This is what caring nurturing resembles. You can help your kids feel and deliver their agonizing recollections, as well. Here are a few ideas:

Try not to respond protectively, recoil, or excuse their aggravation.
Sit with your kids and permit them to feel their feelings and express them.
Permit yourself to feel your kids' excruciating feelings, as well.
Tell your kids you sympathize with their aggravation, hear them, and see them.
Tell your kids you know the previous hurt them, and you're heartbroken.
Tell your kids you won't ever disgrace them for communicating their sentiments.
Tell your youngsters communicating agonizing sentiments about their past is alright.
Pay attention to your kids with everything that is in you.
Offer them your absolute consideration, backing, and love.

Like me, I'm certain you want to have been a more caring guardian previously. Yet, the past is gone, and things have changed. Presently you have the valuable chance to make new, sound, cheerful recollections as a family. Today is an incredible day to begin

How can I be a perfect parent?

Here's the good news. There's no such thing as a perfect parent. Being (or seeming) "perfect" isn't helpful. We're not making it up - science says so, and it's not even new news! In the 1950s, pediatrician Dr. Donald Winnicott introduced the idea that the 'good enough' parent was, in fact, better than the perfect parent. So, let's look at how to be a good parent.

Firstly, what do kids need? A recent analysis of children's views on their well-being and happiness showed that "Feeling loved and having positive, supportive relationships, particularly with friends and family, including having someone to talk to and rely on were consistently stated as a top priority for children to have a happy life."

What qualities make a good parent?

Perhaps you had the world's best parents, or perhaps there are things you'd like to do differently.

If you're constantly researching "parenting 101" or "how to be a parent" then start by using your childhood as a resource.

This can be uncomfortable but self-reflection and awareness are vital to working out those parenting kinks, especially when you find yourself reacting strongly to something your child does or fails to do. When this happens, ask yourself why. For example, if you find that you get frustrated and impatient with your child needing you to walk them through their maths homework every week, take a moment to consider how your parents helped you (or didn't) with schoolwork and how that affected you.

What are the most important parenting skills?

It's hard to provide a definitive list of good parenting qualities – but here are a few that consistently come out on top!

Be positive

One of the top qualities of good parents is positivity. Praising kids doesn't spoil them, and complimenting them on their behavior and achievements only encourages more of the same while building self-esteem. Think about how you react to positive feedback from your boss or a partner.

If your child comes to you with a problem, work through it together. A good parenting approach is to start by finding solutions collaboratively rather than fixing problems for them. This will help your child develop the skills they need to work through future challenges more independently. By contrast, negative input like criticizing or saying things like 'why can't you be more like X' does not help dinnerin any way.

Communicate

As renowned psychotherapist Philipa Perry says "All behavior is communication." Whether your toddler is upset because you gave them a blue spoon (and they were looking forward to choosing the green one – one of the few choices they're allowed to make in a day) or your teenager is starting arguments at the table (because they're learning to think critically and challenge things – an important and valuable skill), what your kids do and say is the best evidence you have for what's going on in their minds and worlds.

If your child tells you that they're unhappy, it doesn't mean you've failed at being a parent, but simply that they need your help in navigating their emotions. Let them know that you're listening to them by acknowledging their unhappiness and letting them express it rather than jumping to solutions.

How we talk to our kids is important. Just because they lack life experience, it doesn't mean we should talk down to them. Sometimes, it's easier for us to shout statements from up high rather than explain what's going on. Remember, even small kids can handle explanations better than you think.

Your child says: I don't want to wear my seat belt! It hurts!

You say: You have to wear your seat belt!

Try saying: I know it can be uncomfortable sometimes but I want you to be as safe as possible while we're in the car – your safety is important to me.

Just as the best leaders acknowledge their faults, the best parents admit when they've made a mistake. If you get something wrong or lose your temper unnecessarily, don't be afraid to address it and apologize. This shows your children that adults mess up too. Again, being perfect helps no one.

Be their safe place

You cannot spoil a child by showing them too much affection. Hugs and declarations of love should be as plentiful as your child needs them to be. Showing unconditional love, even when there's been an issue or an upset will help your child feel more secure.

If they hurt themselves, show sympathy rather than rushing to brush off their pain or discomfort. This won't lead to them manipulating you for comfort or sympathy, and if you find that they do, it's better to find out why rather than deny them their safe place.

Responding to what your child is telling you verbally, physically, and emotionally is paramount to their development. Studies have shown that "Children, especially preterm children, showed faster cognitive growth when mothers were consistently responsive."

In social situations, it can be easy to get waylaid by other people's expectations. Don't force interactions on your child, especially physical ones. Laying down the boundaries of consent and ownership over their bodies can be a scary one to think about but simple to implement if you talk about it openly.

Whether you give your child the mantra of "my body, my choice" or let them choose whether to say goodbye to people with a hug, a high five, or a wave – allowing them to decide how they interact with others is important.

Be consistent

Kids need boundaries and consistency. It's undeniable that you'll need to think about discipline at some point – but remember that the goal is to help them find their way to behavior that isn't harmful to others and learn to regulate their own emotions. Physical discipline such as spanking doesn't work. According to Katie McLaughlin, a clinical psychologist and Harvard professor; "We know that spanking is not effective and can be harmful to children's development and increases the chance of mental health issues."

Rules and routines help kids know what's expected of them and what's coming next. Involving older kids in the development of rules and routines can prevent them from feeling things are being imposed on them unreasonably.

Having boundaries in place doesn't mean you can't be flexible, especially as your kids grow. What was an appropriate rule for a toddler that may be less suitable for a young child? Watching their boundaries grow helps children towards greater independence.

Chapter 3

Form a stronger bond

You've heard it previously: Going through difficult situations is something that can make connections between individuals. The more troublesome the experience, the more seriously holding that might happen. Furthermore, a worldwide pandemic positively qualifies as a condition for reinforcing bonds. The uplifting news is you can anticipate more noteworthy associations and new degrees of closeness with your kin — in all parts of life and work.

Yet, why is holding so huge during tough situations? What it is about shared encounters of torment, that join us so effectively with others? Also, how is holding so basic to our satisfaction and joy? Understanding these can assist you with building bonds, influencing bonds, and keeping up with them over the long run.

Holding Depends On Shared Encounters

By definition, we have a further commitment when we go through extreme encounters. We need to consider the circumstances we're in, consider our reaction, think about influences on others, take care of issues and make do. Each of these causes a critical contribution to numerous reasoning cycles from acquiring attention to building getting it and cultivating compassion.

This more profound mental commitment will in general make tough situations more critical — and our memory is connected with individuals with whom we went through the trouble. We recall the companion who kept in contact. We hold close to the associate who required our help when she was battling. Torment is a common encounter and it is the mix of more profound handling and more paramount conditions which will generally interface with us.

9 Methods for making Areas of strength for Your Youngster

In the current times, an innovation that is considered a gift is likewise one negative component that ruins connections. Dependence on the equivalent has impacted the present youth, and they are probably going to adhere to it for extended periods, leaving their families.

This further riches the relations, and accordingly, guardians can't have serious areas of strength to make with their kids. They endure and den about the equivalent. At times even unforgiving advances are taken by the guardians to draw near to the kid, however, the negativities emerge after so much. Consequently, there is a desperate need that guardians ought to become brilliant and utilize various strategies for dealing with their children and creating security. The most effective ways by which guardians can foster cozy associations with their kids are given underneath.

1. Treat your youngster as really important

The dependence on innovation in addition to the distinction which is now existing among guardians and kids will not disappear soon. Thusly guardians need to comprehend and embrace a consistent methodology for a predictable period to get their children joined. Hence, as a parent, focus on certain you treat your kid as. In this situation, you ought to be accessible to the kid when he wants you, and every one of his interests ought to be heard. As a rule, guardians overlook their youngsters when they are occupied in their public activities, which is positively not right. Thus, how you treat your kid will make your bond develop. Thus, you ought to regard your kid as really important and interface with him in how he needs.

2. Invest energy with your youngster

There are chances that you are a functioning guardian, and afterward, you have other family errands as well. However, this doesn't imply that you can disregard the kid. It is imperative to comprehend that you invest quality energy with your kid and value his prosperity. Ensure consistently you commit the adequate opportunity for your kid. To the more, during the end of the week, you ought to make it a highlight to make espresso or relaxation strolls with your kid similarly with this procedure you would have the option to improve your bond.

3. Switch off the innovation when you both are together

To make your bond solid and cause the kid to understand that connections are more esteemed than anything, ensure you switch off the innovation when you invest energy with him. It ought not to be training from your side, however, you ought to likewise request that your kid do this. Cell phone and virtual entertainment enjoy their benefits, however at that point, eventually, they have specific inconveniences as well. So ensure you and your kid both dispose of online entertainment and different method for innovation when you both are together.

4. Have a go at fostering a well-disposed bond

With the progression and coming up of innovation, things have taken another shape, which was without a doubt very unique during the past. Presently the kids are progressing and have their degree of reasoning. As a parent, you shouldn't simply be a severe dad or mother yet rather have a go at fostering a dear accommodating bond with your child. You ought to cause your child to accept that you are his dearest companion, and you won't leave him at any expense. Indeed, even if you want to guarantee the kid that you will not blow up at his any sort of act; ideally, you will be a steady pal to him. Consequently, when you take on this sort of technique and foster a cordial bond with your kid, you become all the near him, and afterward, things become better.

5. Allow them to have their own space even
You may be fostering an extraordinary bond with your kid, yet you want to comprehend that like each person, the kid likewise needs its own space like each person. To cause your kid to feel great and allow him to unwind, ensure you give him his own space. By space, it isn't simply giving him a decent room, additionally, you want to guarantee that you give the kid quality opportunity to spend inside himself. If you surely don't do that, the kid would feel limited and choked. So you should furnish him with the space he wants.

6. Give them shocks
Your kid is a little bud who, in contrast to different children, hopes to be spoiled. He is paying special attention to all affection and care in addition to hanging tight for minutes when you as guardians would shock him. In this way, to cause your kid to feel cheerful and show him that you understand what he prefers, you ought to without a doubt get shock gifts once in a while for your kid. The astonishment could be little chocolate to a trip pass to a carnival; ensure you do every last bit of it. At the point when you don't get shocks, and the kid sees his friend bunch encountering something very similar, he unquestionably feels horrendous.

7. Be a good example to them
You ought to ensure that you show your kid an energetic character all along. He ought to feel that his dad or mom is astounding and an illustration of how he needs to grow up. At the point when a kid sees your great characteristics and considers you a good example, there are chances of a kid probably getting more joined. Nonetheless, assuming the kid sees that you are an irate individual or consistently continues to yell, the kid would be terrified of you and wouldn't almost certainly get appended to you as a result of the trepidation factor. In this way, it is fundamental to show your right side and allowed the kid to put forth his vocational objectives by getting impacted by you.

8. Have a sound connection with your accomplice
Nurturing doesn't start from the second you converse with the kid and cause him to figure out things. Be that as it may, it at the last begins from the time the kid is conceived. At the point when you have a decent connection with your accomplice, the kid notices something similar and begins fostering a decent bond with you. The improvement of bonds did not depend just on connection, however, starts when you give a solid climate.

9. Engage in the leisure activity of your kid
It is indispensable to comprehend what your kid loves doing. At the point when you are familiar with their side interest, it is not difficult to associate with them. You can seek after it alone and have a good time. For example, assuming your kid loves painting, you can both paint together.

You can show the kid various varieties and their arrangement. With this training, your bond will turn out to be better, and the kid would almost certainly get all the near you. Ensure you find your kid's side interest, and you both do it together when there is spare energy.

For the kid's development and causing them to comprehend family love, fostering serious areas of strength with parents is fundamental. The youngster is a little bud that ought to be suitably supported in the correct heading. Guardians ought to invest the most extreme energy to cause the youngster to feel got and near them. With this training, the youngster would without a doubt foster great relations and bond with their folks.

Chapter4

How to show more love and peace

"You must surrender the existence you arranged, and on second thought, welcome the existence that is sitting tight for you."

"Trust resembles the sun, which, as we venture toward it, creates the shaded area of our weight behind us."

"Disease can't handicap love, it can't break trust, it can't overcome the soul."

"Yesterday is history, tomorrow is a secret, yet today is a gift - that is the reason it's known as 'the present.'"

"Our way isn't delicate grass; it's a mountain way with loads of rocks. In any case, it goes upwards, forward, close to the sun."

"At the point when we long for existence without troubles, advise us that oaks develop further in opposite breezes, and jewels are made under tension."

"Yesterday is gone, tomorrow has not yet come. We have just today, let us start."

"Today won't ever come from now onward. Be a gift. Be a companion. Empower somebody. Get some margin to mind. Allow your words to recuperate, and not injury."

"Don't allow anything to inconvenience you, let nothing terrify you. Everything is passing; God won't ever change. Tolerance gets all things. He who has God doesn't need anything. God alone does the trick."

"God is our asylum and strength, a consistently present assistance in a tough situation."

"Confidence is the bird that sings when the first light is as yet dull."

"My spirit tracks down rest in God; my salvation from him. He is my stone and my salvation; he is my stronghold, I won't ever be shaken."

"God didn't guarantee days without torment, chuckling without distress, or sun without downpour, however, He guaranteed strength for the afternoon, solace for the tears, and light for the way."

"Trust is the capacity to hear the music representing things to come. Confidence is the fortitude to move to it today."

"Harmony. It doesn't intend to be where there is no commotion, inconvenience, or difficult work. It means to be amidst those things regardless and be quiet in your heart."

"In the profundities of winter, I, at last, discovered that inside me there lay a powerful summer."

"Acknowledge what is, let go of what was, and have confidence in what will be."

"Encircle yourself with just individuals who will lift you higher."

"Malignant growth is a word, not a sentence."

"At the point when you go through profound waters, I will accompany you."

Isaiah 43:2

Make an Exceptional Routine Together

This custom doesn't need to be convoluted or costly. The item you are giving your kid is your time. "Perhaps it's a great sleep time saying or schedule, or making their number one treats together on Sundays," says Sadie. "Anything that it is, do it regularly and make it one of a kind and exceptional for every youngster."

This gives them the message they aren't continuously going to be awesome, nobody is, yet that you have confidence they will sort it out and they can deal with this," says, simultaneously, you are likewise constructing their certainty since you are assisting them with tracking down ways of fixing their mix-ups as opposed to stepping in for them. A twofold success!

The truth of the matter is, the disease is a b****. Indeed, even the most hopeful individual, when they let their gatekeeper down and quit attempting to cause every other person to feel hopeful, will tell you. It sucks, easy. So here are my best five ideas on how you can help your companion, adored one, relative, and so on feel more love than dread.

1. Appear. This should be possible in numerous ways, particularly with innovation today. Send a message, an email, or a Facebook message. For hell's sake, on the off chance that you are truly courageous, call the individual. Let them know you are considering them. Let them know you are petitioning God for them. Let them know if they need a punching sack, punch away. Do they require an organization for a physical checkup or output or treatment? Let them know they are in good company in their analysis, treatment, and recuperation. Ask them when their next arrangement is. Appear a way you can.

2. Help the family. The disease requires a decent entire year of regular checkups, medical procedures, therapy, follow-up, recuperation, bloodwork, examinations, and so on. Dealing with this for myself in some cases feels like extra temporary work on top of regular work. The best thing individuals accomplished for me is dealing with my loved ones. They dropped off feasts for my children or gift vouchers for takeout. Simply pick a dinner or an eatery and carry it to your companion/relative/and so on. Try not to ask what you can bring. Simply bring something simple. There was nothing more accommodating to me than this. I was so feeling better to realize that my children and spouse were being taken care of. I've never been so flabbergasted

and thankful to individuals who did this. It permitted me to zero in on recovering, it was good to go to know my loved ones. They additionally dealt with carpool rides, different practices and games, school, and so on. I could zero in on what I assumed.

3. Practice compassion. Attempt to envision what it's preferred to be determined to have a perilous infection. On the off chance that you don't have the foggiest idea what that is like, then, at that point, you presumably don't get the feelings that accompany this. You've never sat in an oncologist's office getting terrible measurements. We most likely kept them from you, because occasionally enduring the worst part of the burden is simply more straightforward. If we are having a blah day, don't think about it literally, or for god sake, shout out and inquire. We will most likely tell you, "Simply having a terrible day with such a large number of fears in my mind. Yet, gratitude for asking." Your asking will show us that however you presumably have no clue about what it's like, you are attempting to comprehend and show a little sympathy in a generally desolate and troublesome street.

4. Treat us similarly. Tune in, because we are going through treatment, it doesn't mean we don't merit being dealt with like any other person. Did we accomplish something that hurt you or ticked you off? We are still individuals, equipped for committing errors and fit for dealing with a showdown on the off chance that we hurt you. The disease didn't out of nowhere enable us to understand brains and fortunes. Our heads and plates are most certainly loaded up with additional things than normal, so kindly shout out or you may never get another chance to speak up. And keeping in mind that you are busy, kindly gripe about the awful bangs your beautician gave you or the way that you destroyed your #1 new pants. This will encourage us. Truly, you likely don't have any desire to discuss every one of the weighty things that disease raises, nor do we! Welcome on the Hollywood tattle or the most recent modest community point of support talk, we will be thankful to have the discussion load eased up.

5. Love us. With this entire s****y "venture," we frequently are left with insecurities. Our bodies sold out us. We are uncertain about scars, uncovered heads, and enlarged injuries. We can't help thinking about how anybody could find us loveable again when we are battling to cherish the new rendition of ourselves. We battle with keeping a light and cushy, super simple rose-colored glasses view on life since we have torn our direction back from the clouded side. Love us at any rate, when we are unreliable and perhaps dim. Perhaps we simply need an update that there is more love on the planet than dread and assuming that we advance the illumination of adoration, we can illuminate any snapshot of dread and murkiness.

However troublesome as it seems to be a malignant growth "warrior," it is likewise difficult being a companion to somebody who is going through a particularly serious and wild finding, treatment, and recuperation. That's what we know. What's more, we will adore you in your snapshots of adoration and dread also.

www.ingramcontent.com/pod-product-compliance
Lightning Source LLC
LaVergne TN
LVHW020547160826
845677LV00015B/4245
9798367573640